I0484702

29 Steps to

AMAZON RICHES

Secrets on how to sell on Amazon, make money online, and make <u>SIX</u> figures!

Praise for 29 Steps to AMAZON RICHES

"If I would have known this information I would have stopped selling on EBay years ago. She showed me her account and she was easily making 3k a month and more with very little effort after setup. If you are an Ebay seller, thinking about selling anything online then you need to get this guide and give yourself. And if you are anything like me and HATE printing invoices, wrapping product and schlepping the boxes to the post office, then your gonna LOVE the part in the bonus. Truly worth the price alone, grab it now!

-Barry Peters

"This is an absolutely brilliant concept! I was initially skeptical when I reviewed it, but I have no doubts that anyone can follow your steps and make an easy $3K / month on auto-pilot and definitely scale the business as well.

For those who are struggling to sell on eBay, grab this guide and sell on Amazon instead"

-Ron H.

"I have just got a copy of the book and I must say that i was living under a rock! As a

powerseller of eBay and got sick of high fees, ever-changing rules, I must say that this book gave me a breath of fresh air.

Thanks and highly recommended!"

-Dee Casp

"I must say that this is very impressive! Her guide delves into this whole other side of Amazon that very few people are aware of. Many people are aware of Amazon's affiliate program, but very few are aware of the myriad options you have to actually sell your own products there. She reveals a little known resource for locating many potentially hot-selling products in her guide, and that alone for me is worth the price of admission for this guide!"

-Paulie Chow

Table of Contents

Why Amazon?

Introduction

Amazon is the first thing I ever made money off of *instantly*. I'm used to months of testing and tweaking before seeing any results so this was a nice change. After about 2 months I was making $3,000 a month in profit and after 4 months of selling I sold $50,000 worth of goods. Shortly after my success I decided it would be a great idea to expand to eBay. HA! eBay was in no way as good as Amazon. There were several things I couldn't stand about them.

1. <u>RULES</u>: out the wazoo! I had my account shut down twice and every representative I talked to had a different reason why. First, I was told that it was because they had concerns about me being a new seller and wanted me to call them. What??! Wouldn't it be easier to just ask me to call them? From there, I got several other explanations that

finally resulted in them wanting three million different kinds of proof that I am who I say I am.

2. <u>BUYERS</u>: The mindset of eBay buyers compared to Amazon buyers is way different. Every eBay buyer is terrified of being scammed so they're suspicious and rude. People would file a PayPal dispute 2 days after ordering without even giving the item a chance to arrive. Wow.

3. <u>MANAGEMENT & LAYOUT</u>: For a newbie, making an eBay website look decent isn't very easy. That's a whole different story with Amazon.

Amazon is better than eBay in every way. It's easier, it's just as well known as eBay, buyers trust Amazon sellers far more than they do eBay, customer service is great, they have an easy to use website creation system, and my favorite of all is that you can create UNLIMITED websites for your monthly membership price.

So let's say that you have 500 items listed in 4 different categories. You can have 4 different websites for the categories instead of jamming it all into one website and looking junky.

Start Your Account

The first thing you'll need, of course is an Amazon storefront account. Most people aren't familiar with this type of Amazon account. The general knowledge about Amazon is that you can be an affiliate but not many people know you can be an actual SELLER on Amazon! And those who know about selling on Amazon don't know about the storefronts. To sign up for the webstore account go to **www.webstore.amazon.com**.

What is a Storefront?

A store front is basically an online store! Amazon store front has easy-to-use software that lets you build websites for your products. It does not matter if you have experience setting up websites or not because it's designed to be extremely easy to use!

Example of a site built on Amazon's Webstore account.

Find a Supplier

Finding what to sell is always the hardest part. Lately, Amazon has gotten a little over crowded right along with eBay. If you've tried to sell anything you've probably noticed that there are 50 other people trying to sell the same thing. When that happens the price of the item keeps going down as everyone fights to have the lowest price. Eventually you get to the point where you're only making a 50 cent profit and that's definitely not enough.

My method has always been to dropship or import.

What is dropshipping? A dropship manufacturer lets you be the middle man in a deal. You can advertise their products and sell them at whatever price you want (within reason, or you won't make any sales). When you make a sale, you order the product from the dropshipper to be sent to the customer. This way you don't have to buy inventory or stock anything. It's quite convenient!

Finding a dropshipper is difficult. There are tons out there and you can find them simply buy googleing "dropshippers". However, so many of the dropshippers out there are not reputable. By that I mean that their prices are not really wholesale, which makes it too difficult to make any money. On top of that, everyone on the planet is trying to sell their items so the competition is too high.

Try Worldwide Brands, the #1 Supplier Resource

I HIGHLY recommend using a company called Worldwide Brands (www.worldwidebrandsproducts.com).They compile a HUGE list of all the reputable doppshippers out there that you can apply to. Many of the companies in their list are very small "mom and pop" sites that you would never know offered dropshipping.

WWB has dropshippers for every niche you can think of, so it's easy to find something that's not over-listed on Amazon. Currently they log over 8,000 dropshippers which they find by attending tradeshows.

From the WWB site:
"*Going to major Wholesale Tradeshows across the United States and around the world is expensive, but that's where you*

find the best Wholesalers. These are the same wholesalers used by professional brick & mortar retail stores. We make sure you connect your online business with only the best factory-direct suppliers."

They also have a certification process for all their dropshippers:
"Our industry leading qualification process ensures that your business is connected to top wholesalers with REAL wholesale prices. We build personal relationships with all of our Wholesalers. They know they are listed in our database and look forward to opening FREE wholesale accounts with our members!"

Worldwide Brands also offers video classes with tons of information on successful dropshipping. The company is truly phenomenal, and they're dedicated towards helping their sellers be successful.

Although WWB does offer a free trial, their one downfall is that the price of a lifetime membership is $299. I'll be the first to admit that it's a high price but also the first to let you know that it's TOTALLY worth it. Aside from the training and high-tech niche research system, you're going to have access to as many products as you'll ever need and WWB is constantly growing. When I joined they had 5,000 dropshippers and that was more than I ever had time to sort through. Now there are 8,000! (You can also become an affiliate if you want to promote their service.)

I highly recommend watching the WWB videos before selecting products. You'll get some great ideas!

Try Other Suppliers

Bulk and Liquidation

Of course there are other ways to sell products than through dropshipping. If you're willing to invest a little cash then your profit margin will be a little bigger if you chose to buy in bulk

Import

One option is to import from China via www.alibaba.com and www.tradekey.com. But beware of the sellers on here. Don't buy anything "name brand" because they're all fakes and you can't sell them on Amazon anyway. However you can get a hold of some nice art, handcrafted items, and generic electronics if those things fit your fancy.

Handmade Crafts

If you are a particularly crafty person and you have some hand made items you can definitely sell them on Amazon. Understand that your sales will be lower for an art item than for something that people need. There is a lot of art on Amazon so buyers have a lot to choose from.

Selling Converted Digital Products

There is a company called Kunaki that takes digital products you've made like DVDs and CDs and converts them to a physical product you can sell. Their work is very high quality and the items look like something you would purchase in the stores. "How To" DVDs sell well on Amazon so if you have the equipment to make some videos take advantage of that!

Start Out on a Budget

If you are one of the people trying to start out your career on a budget then here are some options for you!

Using Free Trials

The advantages of free trials are often over looked. Both Amazon and WWB offer free trials. Clear your schedule as much as possible and then sign up for both free trials. Spend as much time as you possibly can researching and listing products (more on this later). After the trial period, let your WWB account close (make sure they don't auto charge you; If they do, close the account first) while you are listing and waiting for Amazon products to sell. Your Amazon sales should start coming in immediately. Your Amazon products should start selling immediately and if you don't close your Amazon account before the trial is up, they will just take the monthly fee out of your check! If no sales occur just close your Amazon account before they bill you. This way, you've lost no money!

Importing or Handmade Items

As we talked about before, you don't need a membership for importers and you can sell your handmade items. List as many of those items as you can before your free trial with Amazon is up and you should be able to make enough profit to pay for the first month of membership!

Finding a Product on WWB

First, log into your WWB account and click "Find Products Now". A new window will pop up.

Second, enter in the keyword for the product or category you are interested in.

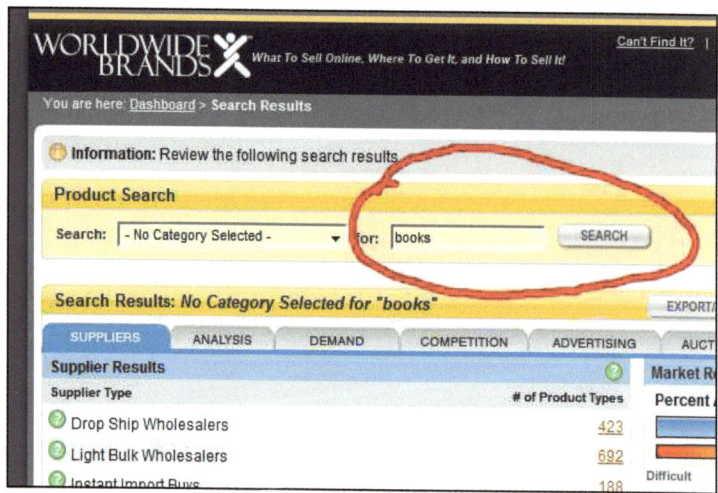

Step 7

Analyze Availability

WWB has a search feature that analyzes your niche/product interest.

Once you have entered your keyword and clicked search, you will see a list of how many dropshippers, wholesalers and liquidators are available in the database.

You will also see a "Market Research Results" box to the left. This calculates your chances of success by finding out how many of those items are listed on the major selling sites like Amazon and eBay!

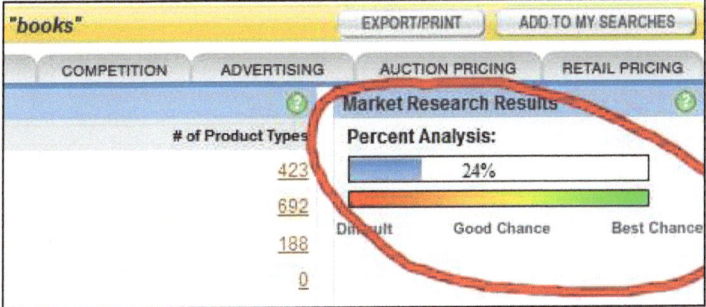

Step  8

Contact Suppliers

Once you have started browsing through
suppliers, you will need to contact them
and request to be a member. When they
accept you, they will give you access to
their product list and prices.

Here is an example of a supplier's page.

Check Competition

After the suppliers accept your application, you can begin to check for competition on the items on Amazon.

For example: if your supplier has the book <u>Talking Heads</u> for the price of $10 then you need to check Amazon.com to see what the going list price is. Of course, if the product is not on Amazon at all then you've got a winner!

If the product IS on Amazon then use this checklist:

1. How many people are selling it?
2. What is the highest and lowest retail price?
3. What are the shipping charges?

Items you list must be able to make a profit of $3 or more

Step 10

List Your Items: Step 1

It is now time to list your items on Amazon!

1. Log into your account at www.sellercentral.amazon.com.
2. Click on the "Inventory" Tab at the top of the page.
3. Click on "Add a Product".

Now, the first set of adding a product is to enter the product name.

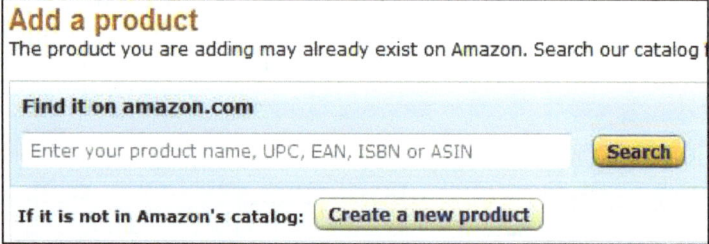

Step **11**

List Your Items: Step 2

If the product is NOT on Amazon then you'll see a page that says "No Products Found". If this is the case, click on Create a New Product.

If a list of products pops up, then look through the products and find the one you are selling. When you find it, click on "Sell Mine"

Manage Your Items

Don't get excited and go overboard! Do one niche at a time and get used to it before adding in another product line. My first 6 months I added in 2,000 products. It didn't take long after that for me to realize that I couldn't manage that many products, and I deleted all but my 100 best sellers.

Stock

YOU alone are responsible for keeping up with inventory which means that you have to be constantly updated with your dropshipper to make sure that they are not out of stock. Amazon has a seller's performance score, and one of the fastest ways to get your points docked is to cancel buyers' orders. They do not like that and neither do the buyers. So don't list more than you can keep updated.

Details

Double check everything when entering in inventory. I can't tell you how many times I entered in the wrong price, wrong shipping, or wrong info. One time I listed a $200 product for $20!

SKUs

Amazon sometimes requires an SKU number for the products which the dropshippers do not supply. However, if you have any luck you can find that same product listed somewhere else with an SKU. If not, write your supplier and find out if they can get you an SKU. Sometimes they can.

Build Your Webstore: Step 1

Pick a Template

For your first site you'll be directed straight to where you pick out your template. For your others, follow these steps.

1. Click on the "Webstore Design" tab at the top of your members page.
2. Click on "Manage Stores".
3. Click on "Create New Store".
4. Pick your template.
5. Choose your store name or upload a logo.
6. Click "1-Click Webstore".

Step 14

Build Your Webstore: Step 2

Adding Inventory

1. Click on the "Webstore Design" tab at the top of the page.
2. Click "Manage Categories".
3. Delete or rename the default categories that are there. Simply click on the category and then click on "delete" or "rename category".
4. After all categories are in place, click the second tab "Assign Products".
5. Click "Scan for new products". This updates the form with your inventory.
6. Check the box by your product then click "Add to Category".

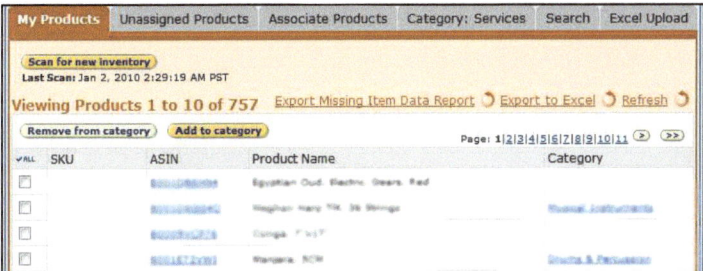

Build Your Webstore: Step 3

Setting up the Template

1. Click on the "Webstore Design" tab at the top of the page.
2. Click on the "Template Management" tab. This is where you edit your website.

The template is set up with "Widgets". You can turn each widget into 1 of 5 things: Text, Image, Product, Category, or a Menu.

All you do is click on the widget you want to edit and chose your option.

For example: See how I added an image widget.

For example: See how I added an image widget.

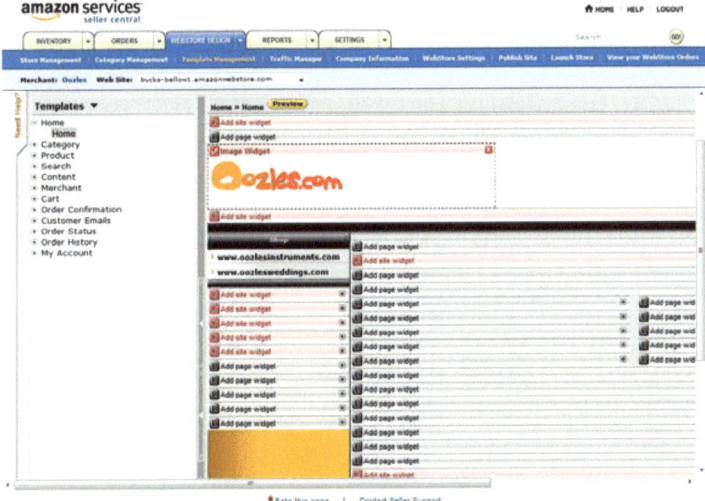

Build Your Webstore: Step 4

Publish Your Site

If you are going to use Amazon's free domain, then all you have to do to publish your new website is to click on the "Publish Site" tab at the top of the page.

However, if you have bought a domain that you wish to use then follow these instructions:

1. Click on the "Webstore Design" tab at the top of the page.
2. Next to "Manage Domain Names" click on "Change Domain Name".
3. Check the "Public Domain" option and click "Save".
4. Next, you will need to change the setting with the website that you bought your domain from.

5. Next, contact technical support for instructions on changing your domain name. Scroll down to the bottom of the page and click on "Contact Customer Support".

Tip: Don't shove all your products into one site. Create sites relevant to what you're selling. For example, put toys on one site, books on one site, and baby stuff on another. Keep it all separated so you can rank better in the search engines.

Learn to Manage Returns

Return Policies

You will get returns for various reasons and you'll have to communicate between the buyer and seller. In order to avoid the most frustration, find out what your dropshipper's return policy is BEFORE you list!
Since you'll have several different dropshippers with several different return policies, your company policy needs to be as strict as possible so you don't get yourself into trouble.

Refunds

Whenever you get a customer's request for a refund you need to do the following:

1. Inform them that they are responsible for return shipment costs

2. Inform them that no refunds can take place until the item has arrived back to the manufacturer, and therefore they MUST get a tracking code to prove that the item has been sent back.
3. Inform the manufacturer of the return and give them the tracking code.

These things are extremely important because manufacturers have often tried to claim that a return shipment never arrived. Amazon does not take kindly to sellers that don't refund buyers and they definitely don't like credit card charge backs. So, unfortunately if a manufacture won't refund you, you will still have to refund your buyers in order to maintain a good rating.

Learn to Order Products

An important part of running a smooth business is know how to process orders.

Speed

Be speedy; as soon as you get an order you should quickly place the order with the dropshipper. The sooner you place the order, the sooner the supplier can ship to the buyer. The last thing you want is late orders.

Payments

Amazon pays you twice a month. You are probably wondering how you'll pay for the items you order for your customers. The best solution is to have a credit card designated to your Amazon business.

Simply place the orders on your credit card. When Amazon pays you, just pay off the card and either pocket the profit or save it to start a reserve account.

I also recommend credit cards so that you are protected against dishonest sellers. You'll want to be able to file a dispute on a purchase if a supplier turns out to be less than reputable.

Get Extra Traffic

Before doing anything be sure to index your site by adding it to the search engines. Go to this link to do it: www.google.com/addurl

Now, Amazon provides plenty of traffic but if you want to generate more then there are ways to do it.

I've found that the best way to get extra clicks to your website is by creating at least 10 link wheels to your products. Many people know how to do this which is good. But when you're promoting products like this, I highly recommend not choosing general product keywords.

Pick one product at a time that you want to promote. Be specific; if you're selling baby cribs then pick one of them you want traffic to.

Good Example: Monterey Convertible Crib (product specific)

Bad Example: Baby cribs (Vague and very high competition)

The conversion rate when you're using a specific product name is very high because you have a customer who is looking for that specific product rather than someone who is just looking for a baby crib in general. Be sure to link directly to your <u>product page</u> and not your main page!

Good Example: www.babycribs.com/monereyconvertiblecrib

Bad Example: www.babycribs.com

Create Linkwheels: Overview

A link wheel consists of at least six web 2.0 sites that are linked in a "wheel" formation. All the Web 2.0 sites link to each other forming the wheel and each 2.0 is also linked to your website product page. *See image below.*

The purpose of a link wheel is to get your website ranked high in search engines. However, there is a dual benefit to linkwheels. I get tons of traffic from the articles in the linkwheels because they rank as well.

Example of a Link Wheel

Image from www.linkwheel.net

Step 21

Create Linkwheels: Step 1

Write or order at least 6 articles. Make sure the article has the name of your product (or keyword) in it at least 3 times.

After the second paragraph put in a line and link to the product page on your website.

See the layout below and note the location of the blue link:

Create Link Wheels: Step 2

Next, submit this article to the 1st Web 2.0 sites. See image of link wheel above.

For example: www.blogger.com

Keep all your login information and the link to your new article. You will need to go back to this page to put another link in later.

Now, you'll need to start on your next article. Put your product link in just like you did last time. Only this time, at the bottom of the article put in a link to your article you submitted to blogger.com.
For example:
www.blogger.com/monereyconvertiblecrib

Keep doing this until you have formed an entire link wheel. Refer to the image on Step 16 for reference if need be

Submit Articles

If linkwheels are too complicated for you, then there is a simpler option.

Write as many articles as you want about your product of choice (the more the better).

Be sure to put in a link to your product page on your website.

Submit your articles to the top article websites.

Popular article sites:
1. www.ezinearticles.com
2. www.goarticles.com
3. www.isnare.com
4. articlebase.com
5. articlecity.com

Sell via Amazon's FBA Program
(Fulfillment by Amazon)

After you have created your Amazon account, you have the option of signing up for Amazon's FBA program. They will store and ship all your items for you and make your business virtually hands free!

Once you have logged into your account, scroll down to the bottom of the page and on the left hand side bar you'll see the option to sign up for FBA.

You might be wondering, what's the purpose of FBA if you're going to be dropshipping?

Well, with FBA you can expand your product line in a different direction. With this method, you'll be able to sell used books, CDs, and DVDs. If you like garage sales, and bargain shopping gets you excited, then this is definitely the career for you!

Ship in Your Items

Once you have signed up for FBA you will need to specify which of your items will be fulfilled by Amazon.

1. Go to your inventory page.
2. Check the box next the product you want to add to FBA.
3. Select the drop down box that says "delete listing".
4. Select "Convert to Amazon Fulfillment".
5. Click "GO".

Once you have done this you'll be directed to the "Send Inventory to Amazon" page.

Provide your "Ship From" address and indicate whether you will be shipping individual or case-packed items.

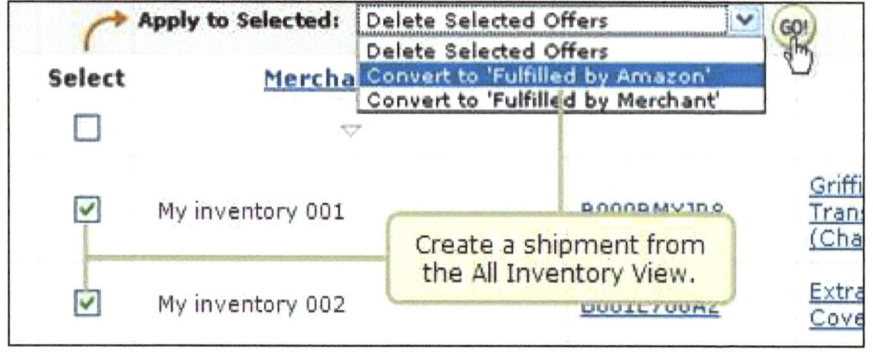

The "Send Inventory to Amazon" page will then show you the location of the fulfillment center to which you have to ship to. Select "Create a New Shipment" then click "Save & Continue.

Sell on FBA

If you've ever done any shopping on Amazon for used items like books, I'm sure you've noticed that there are books selling on there for as low as 1 penny.

Here is an example of one selling for $.50 but with $3.99 shipping:

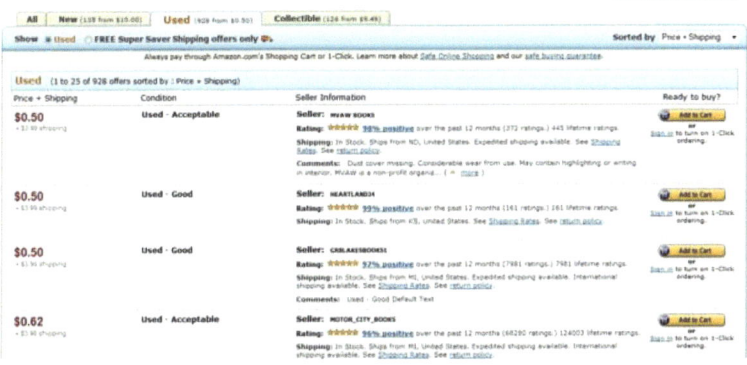

As you can see, there's not much room for profit for these sellers.

However, what they do not know is that when you're a member of the FBA and you sell and item for $3.99 or more, you are eligible for Super Saver and Amazon Prime. This will make your listing appear FIRST on the page!

Understanding FBA's Advantages

There are tons of advantages to using FBA.

- International shipping at no extra cost
- Ability to be #1 on Amazon without cutting profits
- Eligibility to receive free shipping
- FBA offers 1 day shipping to buyers so it's a great incentive

Shipping and Storage

Thanks to Amazon's awesome deal with UPS, you only have to pay $0.20 a pound to ship your goodies to them. However, if you decide to have UPS pick it up then you'll pay and an extra $3 per box. Even then this is still a pretty amazing deal!

Unfortunately it's not free to keep your items at the Amazon warehouse but the cost to keep them there is extremely minimal. They charge $0.45 per cubic foot a month which ends up being about $0.01 to $0.02 per book or small item that you keep there.

So if you have 5,000 books in the warehouse you can expect your monthly cost to be around $46. Not bad to store that many books!

Figuring out your product value

Probably the most time consuming part of selling these used items is sorting them out and figuring out the prices. I'm going to tell you a huge secret to speeding up your pricing issues.

Get an Android phone! With an android phone you can download an application that scans a bar code and tells you how much it's selling

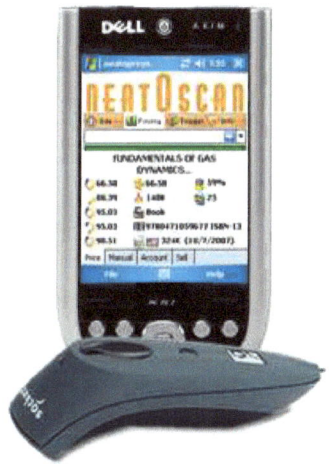

for on Amazon. This is extremely helpful when you're at garage sales, library sales, or anywhere with used books. Not to mention the fact that you have an excuse to buy a cool phone.

If you're not into the phone idea, there are scanners that you can buy that will do exactly what you need.

The best scanner service costs $500 to start up the account and $50 a month after that. Their website is www.neatoscan.com

Shop for Products

Where to shop for the deals

- Library sales
- Garage sales
- Second hand stores
- Used book stores

Super SECRET

If you sign up for Amazon's Super Saver program you are eligible for free shipping on anything over $25. Now, if you're already shopping on Amazon for something, why not add in some 1 cent books to resell? Take the books and list them for $3.99 so that you're eligible for the free shipping and you've just made some super easy profit!!

Recognize Your Potential!

No matter how easy it is to make money, you still won't make it unless you put forth the effort!

I made $4,875 in my second month! And this is only HALF the month's payment! My next payment was $2,000 for the month! So as you see, there are no limits except the ones you create. You could be self-employed in just a few months! Take the next steps towards your success now!

List of Web 2.0 Sites to Use for Linkwheels

USfreeads.com
Hubpages.com
Blog.com
Wordpress.com
Zimbio.com
Wikispaces.com
Blogspot.com
Wetpaint.com
Quizilla.com
Google Knol
MSN Spaces
Tripod.com
Google Sites
Webs.com
Vox.com
Livejournal.com
Xanga.com
Ning.com
Friendster.com
Jimdo.com
Zoho.com
Gather.com

Thoughts.com
Dairyland.com
Terapad.com
Insanejournal.com
Onsugar.com
Blogetery.com
Easyjournal.com
Nexo.com
Atwiki.com
Zoomgroups.com